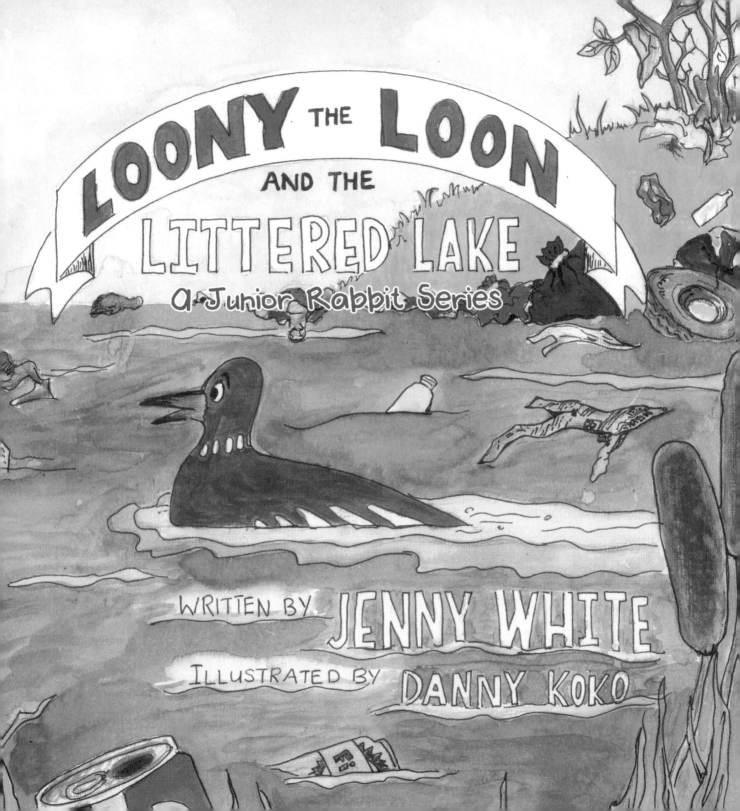

LOONY THE LOON AND THE LITTERED LAKE

A Junior Rabbit Series

WRITTEN BY JENNY WHITE

ILLUSTRATED BY DANNY KOKO

AuthorHouse™
1663 Liberty Drive
Bloomington, IN 47403
www.authorhouse.com
Phone: 1 (800) 839-8640

Published by AuthorHouse 05/02/2016

ISBN: 978-1-5049-1056-9 (sc)
ISBN: 978-1-5049-1057-6 (e)

Print information available on the last page.

Any people depicted in stock imagery provided by Thinkstock are models,
and such images are being used for illustrative purposes only.
Certain stock imagery © Thinkstock.

This book is printed on acid-free paper.

authorHOUSE®

WHEN LOONY RETURNED HOME FROM JUNIOR'S SURPRISE BIRTHDAY PARTY, IT WAS ALREADY DARK AND HE WAS EXHAUSTED. HE HAD REALLY HAD A WONDERFUL TIME THERE. THE FISH PIE THAT MAMA RABBIT HAD MADE FOR HIM FOR HELPING THEM SURPRISE JUNIOR HAD BEEN DELICIOUS! HE WAS SO TIRED, HE WENT RIGHT TO SLEEP.

WHEN HE AWOKE THE FOLLOWING MORNING, WHAT HE SAW MADE HIM VERY VERY SAD. THE LAKE HE LOVED SO MUCH, AND WHERE HE AND HIS FRIENDS LIVED AND PLAYED WAS LITTERED WITH ALL TYPES OF TRASH.

THERE WERE SODA CANS EVERYWHERE. BROKEN BOTTLES, PLASTIC GROCERY BAGS, PAPER, CIGARETTE BUTTS, PLASTIC RINGS OFF SODA CANS, DISPOSABLE DIAPERS AND LOTS AND LOTS OF OTHER STUFF!

CARELESS PEOPLE HAD BEEN MAKING A MESS, WHERE THE ANIMALS BUILT THEIR NESTS.

THEY SEEMED TO BE UNCARING, GARBAGE BEARING, PAPER TEARING, DEBRIS SMEARING, MESS MAKING, BOTTLE BREAKING PERSONS WHO CARED VERY LITTLE ABOUT THEIR ENVIRONMENT, OR ABOUT THE ANIMALS LIVING IN IT.

AS LOONY SAT LOOKING AT THE LITTER, HE SAW A CAR TRAVELING ON THE ROAD ABOVE. SOMEONE IN THE CAR ROLLED THE WINDOW DOWN AND THREW TRASH OUT OF IT!

WHILE WATCHING ALL THIS, HE HEARD A SMALL HOARSE, "QUACK, QUACK." HE TURNED AND SAW DANA DUCK FLOATING THROUGH THE WATER WITH A PLASTIC SODA CAN CARTON RING AROUND HER NECK!

LOONY IMMEDIATELY RAN TO HER RESCUE. HE TRIED WITH ALL HIS MIGHT TO GET IT OFF, BUT COULDN'T. HE NEEDED TO FIND BUCK THE COCK-EYED BEAVER AS QUICKLY AS POSSIBLE! HE KNEW BUCK WOULD BE ABLE TO GNAW THROUGH THE PLASTIC, JUST AS HE HAD GNAWED THROUGH JENNY THE SQUIRREL'S FRONT DOOR AFTER SHE ACCIDENTALLY LOCKED HERSELF OUT.

LOONY FLEW TO SUGAR LAKE WHERE HE KNEW BUCK SOMETIMES
HUNG OUT WITH HIS FRIEND LIZZIE THE LIZARD, BUT BUCK
WASN'T THERE AND LIZZIE HAD NO IDEA WHERE HE WAS.

LOONY CONTINUED TO FLY AROUND UNTIL HE SAW BETTY BIRD.
HE WAS GOING TO STOP AND ASK HER IF SHE HAD SEEN BUCK, BUT
AS HE GOT CLOSER, HE COULD TELL SOMETHING WAS SERIOUSLY
WRONG. BETTY WAS FRANTICALLY HOPPING ALL AROUND TRYING
TO GET HER BEAK OUT OF AN EMPTY GLASS MAYONNAISE JAR!

LOONY TRIED TO PULL THE JAR OFF HIS FRIEND'S BEAK BUT IT WAS MORE THAN HE COULD DO ALONE. SO OFF HE FLEW TO CONTINUE HIS QUEST TO FIND HELP.

HE FLEW TO TAMMY THE TURTLE'S HOUSE AND WHAT HE SAW
THERE WAS VERY FRIGHTENING! ONE OF HER BABY TURTLES HAD
SOMEHOW GOTTEN ONE OF THE PLASTIC RINGS FLOATING IN
THE LAKE CAUGHT AROUND HER ENTIRE BODY!

LOONY WAS IN DISTRESS. HE COULDN'T UNDERSTAND WHY THERE WERE SO MANY UNCARING, PAPER TEARING, DEBRIS SMEARING, MESS MAKING, BOTTLE BREAKING PERSONS WHO COULD PASS BY TRASH CANS AND INSTEAD OF PUTTING THEIR RUBBISH IN THERE, WOULD CHOOSE TO THROW IT ON THE GROUND.

HE FLEW ALL OVER THE LAKE UNTIL HE WAS TOTALLY EXHAUSTED.
HE STILL HADN'T FOUND BUCK AND IT WOULD BE DARK SOON.

LOONY SWOOPED DOWN AND LANDED. HE HADN'T FOUND BUCK, HIS FRIENDS WERE STILL IN TROUBLE AND HE DIDN'T KNOW WHAT TO DO.

AS HE SWAM AROUND TRYING TO THINK, HE THOUGHT HE HEARD A SMALL VOICE WHISPERING HIS NAME.

HE TURNED TOWARD THE SOUND AND COULDN'T BELIEVE HIS EYES. IT WAS BUCK! HE SWAM OVER TO HIM FLAPPING HIS WINGS WILDLY! "BUCK, WHERE HAVE YOU BEEN, I'VE BEEN LOOKING ALL OVER FOR YOU?"

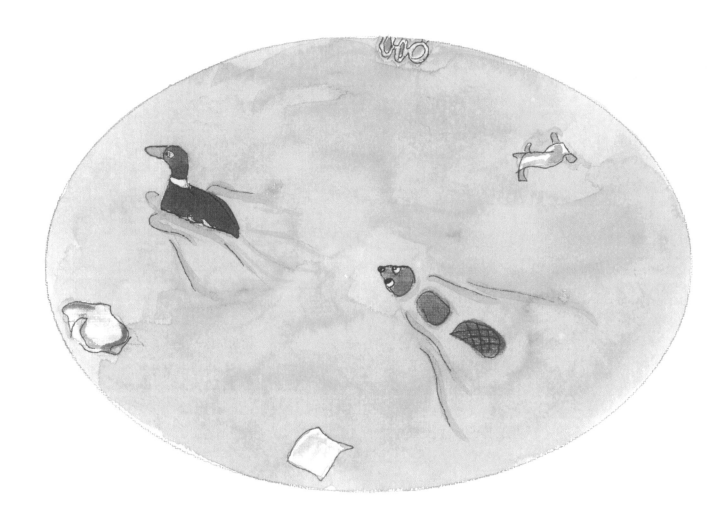

BUT BEFORE BUCK COULD ANSWER, LOONY YELLED, "FOLLOW ME!"
HE LED HIM UP THE LAKE TO TAMMY'S TINY BABY TURTLE.

WHEN BUCK SAW THE TINY TURTLE, HE KNEW EXACTLY WHAT TO DO. HE GNAWED THE PLASTIC OFF THE SMALL BODY. AS SOON AS IT WAS FREE, THE BABY TURTLE QUICKLY JUMPED INTO THE WATER! TAMMY SHOUTED, "THANK YOU, BUCK" AS SHE DOVE INTO THE WATER BEHIND HER TINY BABY TURTLE.

LOONY THEN LED BUCK FURTHER UPSTREAM TO DANA THE DUCK,
WHO ONCE SHE SAW BUCK, BEGAN TO THRASH ABOUT WILDLY!
LOONY HAD TO GO OVER AND CALM HER DOWN BEFORE BUCK
COULD BEGIN TO GNAW AT THE PLASTIC AROUND HER NECK. ONCE
SHE WAS FREED, DANA BEGAN TO QUACK VERY LOUDLY! "QUACK,
QUACK, QUACK!" (WHICH MEANT THANK YOU IN DUCK LANGUAGE).

BETTY BIRD WAS THE LAST ONE TO BE FREED. THIS WAS NOT GOING TO BE AS SIMPLE AS THE OTHERS. HER BEAK WAS STUCK IN A JAR! LOONY FLEW BACK TO BETTY BIRD, WHO WAS STILL FLAPPING HER WINGS IN AN ATTEMPT TO GET HER BEAK OUT OF THE MAYONNAISE JAR.

WITH LOONY AND JENNY GATHERED AROUND TO HELP, BETTY CLIMBED ON TOP OF BUCK'S NEST. THEY HELD ON TO EACH OTHER AND TO BETTY. BUCK, SEEING A SMALL SPACE BETWEEN HER BEAK AND THE MOUTH OF THE JAR, TOOK A TWIG AND CAREFULLY PUT IT INTO THAT SPACE. THEN LOONY AND JENNY GOT BEHIND BETTY AND PULLED WITH ALL THEIR STRENGTH. BETTY'S BEAK CAME OUT WITH A 'WHOOSH!' SHE THANKED BUCK AND FLEW UP TO HER NEST.

AS THE SUN SET DOWN ON THE LAKE AND THE SHADOWS BEGAN TO DANCE ON THE WATER, LOONY FINALLY GOT A CHANCE TO ASK BUCK WHERE HE HAD BEEN.

BUCK TOLD LOONY THAT HE HAD BEEN REPLACING TWIGS ON HIS HOUSE WHEN HE HAD ACCIDENTALLY GOTTEN A CIGARETTE BUTT, WHICH HAD FALLEN ON ONE OF THE TWIGS, CAUGHT IN HIS THROAT. HE HAD GONE TO THE ANIMAL HOSPITAL TO HAVE IT REMOVED.

LOONY WAS VERY SAD WHEN HE HEARD THAT. IN ONE DAY FOUR OF HIS FRIENDS HAD BEEN HURT BY THE CARELESSNESS OF PEOPLE LITTERING. AS HE SAT AND WATCHED THE MOON TAKE THE SUN'S PLACE IN THE SKY AND THE SHADOWS AS THEY CONTINUED TO DANCE ON THE WATER, HE WONDERED WHAT WOULD EVENTUALLY BECOME OF HIM AND HIS FRIENDS IF THE LITTERING DIDN'T STOP? WOULD IT BE...The end?

Printed in the United States
By Bookmasters